The Adventures of
ABNEY & TEAL

Busy Days
Sticker Activity Book

Joel Stewart

WALKER
ENTERTAINMENT

Abney and Teal and their friends live on an island. Abney likes gardening. Teal loves bright colours. Bop lives in the water. Neep tunnels underground. The Poc-Pocs stand on top of each other. Toby Dog plays his accordion from across the water.

Put stickers of everyone on the island.

Who would like stickers of these things?

Abney is tidying up the hut. Use the stickers and help him put everything back on the shelves.

Everything will be so clean!

Abney and Teal are working in the garden.
Teal wants to plant some flowers and
Abney wants to water his cabbages.

Use the stickers to make sure they
have everything they need.

Abney and Teal are counting together. "Good things come in threes," says Abney.

How many are there of each of these?

Use the stickers to make sure there are three of each of these.

cheep

quack!

One, two, three...

Abney, Teal, Bop and Neep are fishing in the lake.
Can you untangle their fishing lines? Use the stickers
to fill in the gaps and show what they have caught.

Bop has caught a

Teal has caught a

Neep has caught a

Abney has caught a

He, he, he!

It's a treasure hunt! Can you help Abney find these things?

Use the stickers to give everyone a medal for doing so well. Remember you need one too!

The Poc-Pocs are having a games day.
How many are there in the race?

Now they are having a tug-of-war. Use the stickers
to make sure there are the same number of
Poc-Pocs on each side of the rope.

The Poc-Pocs and Neep are seeing who is the tallest.
Use the stickers to line them up from the
shortest to the tallest.

Teal is making a delicious picnic. Can you spot five differences between the two pictures?

A

Use the stickers to make the pictures look the same.

B

Abney is making his favourite food. Fill in the gaps with stickers and help him make the perfect porridge.

Abney puts the _____ into

the _____ and adds _____

He heats the pan and stirs the mixture

with a _____

When it bubbles, he puts the porridge

into a _____

Delicious!

It's Bop's birthday. Use the stickers to help decorate the island with bunting and balloons. Don't forget to give everyone a party hat. Make sure that Bop is blowing lots of birthday bubbles.

Abney is looking through his telescope. What can he see? Put a sticker in each box to show what he is looking at.

Bop is busy blowing bubbles in the lake.
Can you spot five differences between the pictures?

A

B

Teal has found a new umbrella and wants to decorate it.
Use the stickers to make it bright and colourful.

Abney and Neep are reading about the stars.
Use the stickers to finish the jigsaw.

Abney, Teal and Neep are looking at the night sky. How many shooting stars can they see? Use the stickers to decorate the sky with more stars. It's a cold night. Use the stickers to give Abney his scarf and Teal her woolly hat.

23

The Adventures of
ABNEY & TEAL

Also available:

ABNEY & TEAL MIX &
MATCH CARD GAME

ABNEY & TEAL BEAN TOY
ASSORTMENT

ABNEY & TEAL 24 PIECE
FLOOR PUZZLE

ABNEY & TEAL
WOODEN DOMINOES

ABNEY RAG DOLL

TEAL RAG DOLL

TALKING NEEP PLUSH

Text by Stella Gurney
Illustrations by Joel Stewart and Davide Arnone

First published 2014 by Walker Entertainment
an imprint of Walker Books Ltd, 87 Vauxhall Walk, London SE11 5HJ

2 4 6 8 10 9 7 5 3 1

This book has been typeset in AbneyandTeal font

Printed in China

British Library Cataloguing in Publication Data: a catalogue record for this book is available from the British Library

ISBN 978-1-4063-5657-1

www.walker.co.uk